THE DINO QUIZ BOOK

THE DINO QUIZ BOOK

Calling all Dinosaur Experts!

by Miriam Schlein

Illustrated by
Nate Evans

Scholastic Inc.
New York   Toronto   London   Auckland   Sydney

ISBN 0-590-48121-5

12 11 10 9 8 7 6 5 4 3 2 1   5 6 7 8 9/9 0/0

Printed in the U.S.A.   40

First Scholastic printing, January 1995

The author thanks Dr. E. H. Colbert

How much do you know about

DINOSAURS?

Are you a dinosaur expert?
Let's see.
What's your DIno-Q?

How many of these dino-questions
can you answer?

Is this true? Or false?

Dinosaurs could not live to be more than about 100 years old.

FALSE!

Some dinosaurs could probably live longer than that.

How do we know?

We can tell how old a tree is by the number of growth rings in its trunk.

growth rings

Dinosaurs also have growth rings on their teeth and bones. These seem to show that some dinosaurs — especially the big ones — might have had a lifespan of 300 years. Maybe more.

_____

Some dinosaurs had more than 1,000 teeth.

True? Or false?

If you said **TRUE**, you're right. A duckbill dinosaur could have up to 1440 teeth! But not all at the same time.

Duckbills ate tough food — things like pine needles and twigs.

Teeth get worn down after a while, chewing on tough stuff like that. But, as one bunch of duckbill teeth wore out, new teeth grew in to take their place.

A duckbill had six extra layers of teeth ready to take over the job of chewing. This might add up to 1440 teeth. Neat system!

How do we know this?

Duckbill skulls show layers of reserve teeth.

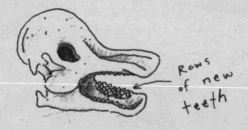

Rows of new teeth

Do you know what animals today also have a tooth replacement system?

Elephants!

When an elephant's teeth get worn down, new teeth from the back of the jaw push forward and take their place. The old worn teeth move forward and break off in pieces.

When the sixth set of teeth is worn down, there are no more. The old elephant can't chew anymore and will die of starvation.

Duckbills had 45 to 60 small teeth in each jaw, left, right, upper, and lower. Elephants have one big tooth per jaw at a time. Once in a while, two. But never more.

Crocodiles and sharks have a tooth replacement system, too.

Dinosaur fossils have been discovered in every part of the world except in Antarctica. For this reason, we do not know whether they ever lived there.

True? Or false?

FALSE!

Until the 1980s, the answer would have been true.

Then . . . FLASH NEWS BULLETIN!

1986: A crew of Argentinian paleontologists find an ankylosaur — an "armored" dinosaur — in Antarctica.

1989: American paleontologists make another dinosaur find in Antarctica — this one a hypsilophodont.

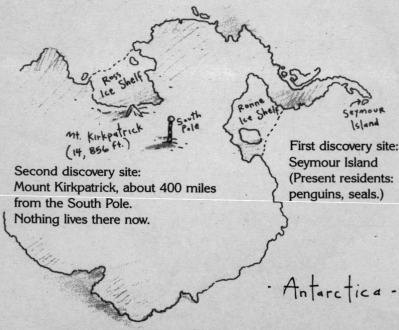

Second discovery site:
Mount Kirkpatrick, about 400 miles from the South Pole.
Nothing lives there now.

First discovery site:
Seymour Island
(Present residents: penguins, seals.)

1991: A different kind of dinosaur was found 400 miles from the South Pole. It was a 25-foot-long flesh-eater, with sharp teeth, strong jaws, and a bony crest on its head. It is named *Cryolophosaurus* — frozen crested reptile.

Cryolophosaurus

So — now we know there *were* dinosaurs in Antarctica.

The first dinosaurs in Antarctica had to swim long distances to get there. This is how we know that dinosaurs — at least some of them — must have been powerful swimmers.

True? Or false?

FALSE.

They did not have to swim.
They got there by walking.

How could they *walk* to a continent surrounded by water?

In early dinosaur times, the continents were not separated the way they are now. They were all connected to one another. It was one big supercontinent. We call it *Pangaea* ("All Earth"). Dinosaurs could walk to every part of the earth. And they did. It was only later in dinosaur times that the continents "drifted" apart.

Did you know that the continents are still moving? But don't worry. It's only a few inches a year. This process is called Continental Drift, or plate tectonics.

The Approximate Positions of the Continents During The Mesozoic Era

Pangaea

200 Million Years Ago

Laurasia

Gondwanaland

150 Million Years Ago

North America   Eurasia

Africa

South America

India

Australia

Antarctica

70 Million Years Ago

Many paleontologists agree that the Antarctic dinosaurs may have had to be covered with fur to keep them warm in the ice and snow.

True? Or false?

FALSE.

In the time of the dinosaurs, Antarctica was not a cold place covered with ice, the way it is now. It was a warm, tropical land.

How do we know that?

Fossils of ferns and other tropical plants and trees have been found in Antarctica. (Before it drifted southward, this chunk of land was closer to the equator than it is now.)

Supersaurus, estimated to be 82 to 98 feet long, and 54 feet high, is the biggest dinosaur ever discovered.

True? Or false?

Well, it *was* true. For a while. But not for long . . .

Supersaurus:
Discoverer: Jim Jensen
Discovery date: 1972
Where: Dry Mesa Quarry, Colorado

. . . because a few years later, in the same part of Colorado, Jim Jensen found a dinosaur even bigger — one that was probably 100 feet long, maybe more. He named this one *Ultrasaurus*.

Does this mean that *Ultrasaurus* now holds the record as the biggest dino ever?

NO.

In the 1980s, in New Mexico, a new dino-find was made. It was bigger than Super... bigger than Ultra. Here was the new record-breaker! Paleontologist David Gillette judged its size might have been about 150 feet long! What can you name a giant like that? He named it *Seismosaurus* — "earth-shaker."

Seismosaurus possibly tipped the scales at something like 180 tons. That's 360,000 pounds!

Will anything bigger ever be found?
Who knows...?

Scientists tell us all dinosaurs were brown or gray in color.

True? Or false?

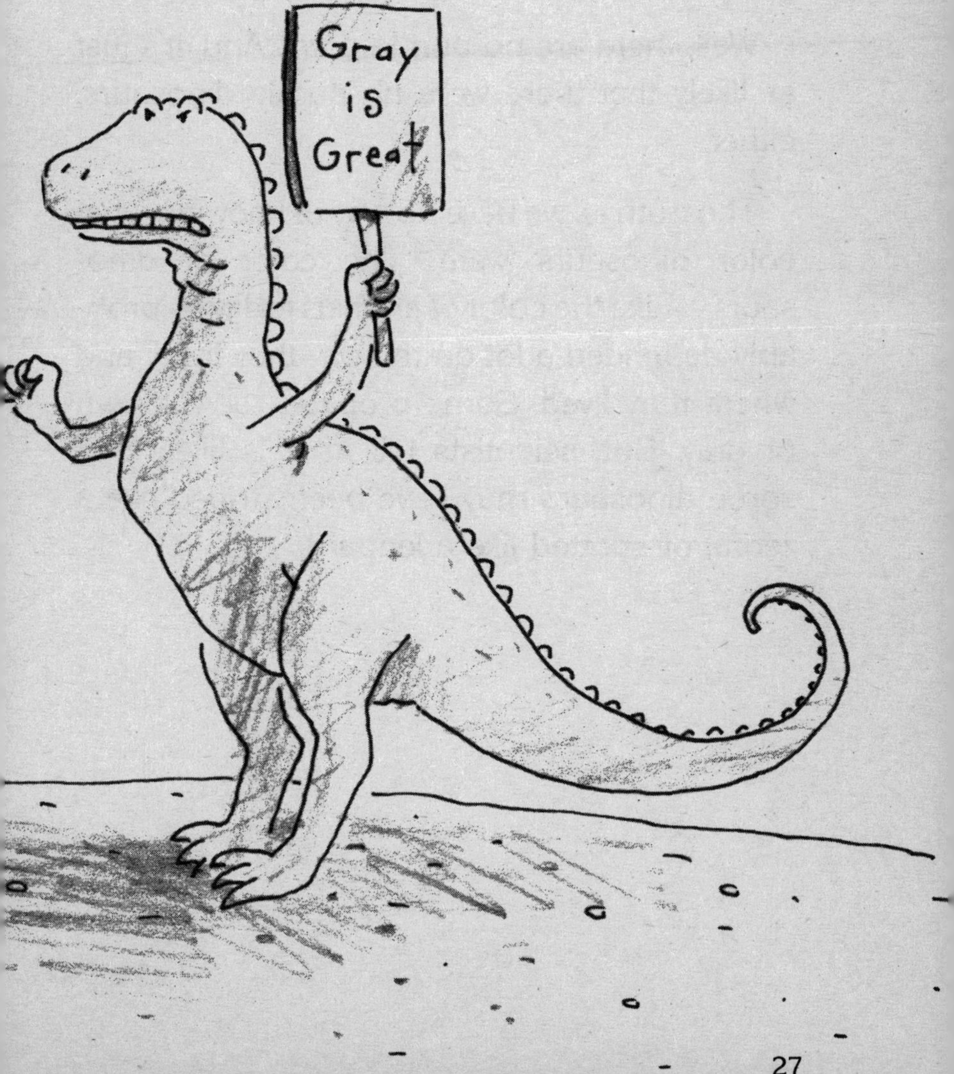
Gray is Great

FALSE.

Do you know the poem that starts:
"I never saw a purple cow
I never hope to see one . . ."?

Well, there are no purple cows. And, it's just as likely that there were no purple dinosaurs, either.

The truth is, we have no way of knowing what color dinosaurs were. The color of dinosaurs — like the color of animals today — probably depended a lot on the way they lived, and where they lived. Some probably *were* brown or gray. But, scientists tell us it is likely that some dinosaurs may have been striped like a zebra, or spotted like a leopard.

Protective coloration would help them blend
in amid leaves and shadows, so as not to be
seen by an enemy.

It is not impossible that some dinosaurs were brightly colored as some reptiles are today.

But probably not purple.
Then again . . . who knows?

(The Sonora Mountain King Snake has red, black, and white bands. The Corn Snake is bright orange.)

Why did *Diplodocus* swallow stones?

(a) to exercise his teeth?

(b) to help digest his food?

(c) to weigh him down, so he wouldn't
    blow away in a wind?

The answer is: (b) to help digest his food.

Diplodocus was one of the giant plant-eating dinosaurs we call sauropods. But it had weak, small teeth, teeth that could not do a good job of chewing all the food that this 87-foot-long giant needed. If *Diplodocus* swallowed stones, they would help to grind up the food in its stomach — a job that weak little teeth could not do.

What gives scientists this idea?

Many times smooth stones have been found jumbled up with sauropod remains — too often to seem just a coincidence. We call them *gastroliths* — "stomach stones."

It's not such a strange idea. Birds swallow pebbles to help grind their food.

The gastrolith idea made sense to some scientists. Others said the idea was hogwash, and that the stones were worn down smooth by a stream, and not because they were grinding against each other in the stomach of a sauropod.

For a long time there was no solid evidence to back up the gastrolith idea.

Now there is some very solid evidence that sauropods *did* swallow stones.

What is this evidence? At the *Seismosaurus* dig in the 1980s, David Gillette found lots of gastroliths. Enough to fill up 10 buckets.

Exactly where did he find these "stomach stones"?

He found them *inside* the rib cage of *Seismosaurus,* which means the stones were inside the stomach and intestines of the sauropod when it died. This is pretty definite evidence that they were swallowed, isn't it? How else would they have gotten there?

It seems likely that *Seismo* — being so big — could probably swallow stones as big as a basketball.

True? Or false?

FALSE.

Most of the stomach stones found in what would have been *Seismosaurus*'s gut were more like the size of a peach. The biggest stone found by Gillette was about 4 inches across — about as big as a small grapefruit.

This big stone was found high up, higher than all the other stones, in what would have been the dinosaur's throat. In fact, Gillette thinks it is possible that this grapefruit-size stone was too big to go down the dinosaur's throat and the dinosaur choked on it. That could have been what caused this dinosaur to die!

**Some dinosaurs were nocturnal —
active at night.**

True? Or false?

TRUE.

Dromiceiomimus, one of the "ostrich dinosaurs," and *Troödon,* with its "steak-knife" teeth, were flesh-eating dinos who probably hunted by night.

How do we know?

By their eyes. These dinosaurs had extra-large eyes. Large eyes are generally a feature of a creature that is active at night — like the owl.

Many dinosaurs had sails on their backs, which helped them pick up speed as they sailed around on inland lagoons.

True? Or false?

FALSE. And false again.

Very few dinosaurs had a "sail." And the ones that did, did *not* use it for cruising around inland lagoons.

If not for sailing, what good is a sail on a dinosaur?

1. A sail could help protect the dinosaur by making it harder for an attacker to bite into its neck.

2. The sail could help keep the dinosaur warm. Blood vessels in the sail were warmed by the sun, then circulated through the dinosaur's body later on, when the sun went down.

The first dinosaurs were very big. As millions of years went by, they got smaller and smaller.

True? Or false?

FALSE! It was just the opposite.

The first dinosaurs were very small. *Eoraptor*, one of the first dinosaurs, was three feet long, and weighed about 25 pounds. Some other early dinosaurs were *Staurikosaurus* (six feet long, weight about 66 pounds), *Coelophysis* (eight feet long, weight about 65 pounds), and *Saltopus* (two feet long, weight about two pounds).

These mini-dinos appeared in Middle Triassic times. (Triassic Period: 248–213 million years ago.)

The real giants of the dinosaur world came along later. The giants appeared mostly late in the Jurassic Period (213–144 million years ago) and lived right on through the Cretaceous Period (144–65 million years ago) till the end of dinosaur times.

Triassic Period | Jurassic Period | Cretaceous Period

248   213   144   65

- Millions of years ago -

Remember this: Though all early dinosaurs were small, not *all* later dinosaurs were big. *Troödon* (Late Cretaceous) was six feet long. *Struthiomimus* (Late Cretaceous) was 11 feet long.

All dinosaurs were more or less slow-pokes. No dinosaur, for example, could run as fast as an elephant.

True? Or false?

FALSE!

Struthiomimus, an "ostrich dinosaur," was a speed runner and probably could have beaten an elephant in a race. Not that elephants are slowpokes. The top speed of an elephant is 25 mph. Ostrich dinosaurs could probably run 35–40 mph — maybe even faster.

How do we know that? No one ever clocked a dinosaur running.

We know by their tracks. When they take long steps, and the track is narrow, this shows a fast speed.

By examining fossil dino-tracks, and knowing how long the legs were (we can tell this by the size of their leg bones), scientists can figure out — more or less — how fast the dinosaur was running.

Another way of judging dinosaur speed is by comparing the body structure of the dinosaur with that of a living animal (the speed of which we *can* clock). Ostrich dinosaurs were built a lot like ostriches. (That's why they have this name.) And ostriches are really fast runners, with a top speed of 40 mph or more. (Their stride is up to 20 feet.) Ostrich dinosaurs could probably run just as fast.

There were once gigantic flying dinosaurs with a wingspan of 50 feet!

True? Or false?

FALSE!

Did you ever hear the saying, "If a pig had wings, it could fly"? It's the same with dinosaurs. There never was a flying dinosaur.

There *was* a gigantic flyer in dinosaur times. Its name is *Quetzalcoatlus*. It had a wingspan of 50 feet. But *Quetzalcoatlus* was a pterosaur — a winged reptile. It was not a dinosaur.

We often read about *Archaeopteryx* in dinosaur books. *Archaeopteryx* did have wings, and probably could fly. But *Archaeopteryx*, because it had feathers, is considered to be a bird, and not a dinosaur.

Besides, *Archaeopteryx* was no giant. It was more like the size of a raven.

It has recently been proven that the dinosaur *Dilophosaurus* was particularly dangerous because it was able to spit poisonous venom at its enemies.

True? Or false?

This is FALSE.

There is no basis for the idea that a dinosaur could or would spit at its enemies.

The bigger the dinosaur, the bigger the eggs.

True? Or false?

FALSE.

The biggest dinosaur eggs ever found were 12 inches long and 10 inches wide. They are thought to be eggs of the 40-foot-long sauropod *Hypselosaurus*. But scientists tell us even if a dinosaur were twice the size of *Hypselosaurus*, its eggs would still not have been much bigger. Because 12″ × 10″ is just about the biggest any egg could be.

Why is that?

If an egg were bigger than that, the shell would have to be too thick for the baby — even a dinosaur baby! — to peck its way out. A thicker shell would also be too thick for oxygen to get through to the baby embryo inside.

———————

Some paleontologists think it is possible that some dinosaurs may have had two hearts — one in the body, and one partway up the neck.

True? Or false?

It's TRUE.

Why would they think that?

It's because of the "giraffe problem."

A giraffe's head is about eight feet higher than its heart. Is this a problem? Yes. It's very hard for a heart to pump blood up so high to the brain. The giraffe has a series of valves that helps its blood to flow upward. Even so, giraffes have very high blood pressure.

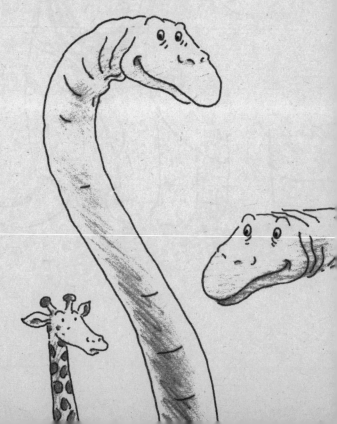

A sauropod head might have been 20 feet or more higher than the body. How could the blood keep flowing "uphill" so far? If the sauropod had an extra heart, maybe halfway up the neck, it would help boost the blood way up to the brain. It's an unusual thought.

Then again, dinosaurs were unusual animals!

In fact, in 1992 two heart specialists wrote a paper saying that the sauropod *Barosaurus* may have had eight hearts to boost the flow of blood upward through that long, high neck to its brain!

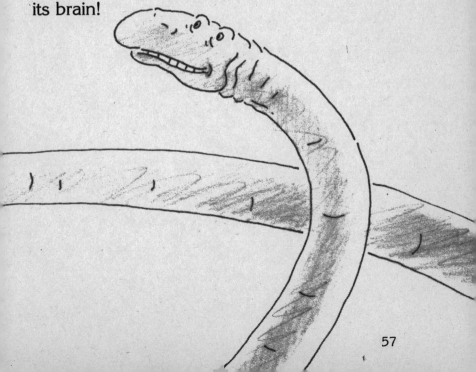

If one dino-fossil is found buried at a lower level than another, we can be certain that the lower one lived at an earlier time.

Is that true?

It is very likely to be true. But we cannot be certain.

Why not? Doesn't "lower down" mean it's from an older time?

It usually does. But not always. Sometimes, due to pressure and shifting of rock below the Earth's surface, a particular area can be pushed upward, and end up higher than the layer that was once above it. The layers are pushed out of order.

Sometimes you can see this in exposed cliffs showing rock of prehistoric times. The layers become uneven. This kind of break is called a geologic *fault.* This is why a deeper fossil is not always older. Usually it is . . . but not always.

Fossil bones get heavier as millions of years go by.

True? Or false?

It's TRUE.

Why is that?

Bone is made up of hard parts and softer parts. When a dinosaur dies, and the bones are buried, the hard bony parts remain. But the softer parts — things like the sugar, the fat,

which are also part of bone — disappear, leaving blank spaces. These spaces are then filled in by minerals, such as quartz, which are heavier than the original material. This is how, as time goes by, the fossil becomes heavier.

When a dino fossil is removed from the ground, dino-hunters put shellac on it, or sometimes even nail polish, to make it more attractive for when it is shown in a museum.

Is that true?

Well, yes . . . and no.

They *do* put shellac, nail polish, or some coating surface on a fossil right away. But not to make it more attractive! They do it because otherwise, when the bone is suddenly exposed to the air after all those millions of years, it might crumble into bits. Which would be a shame. Wouldn't it?

There were lots of big trees around
when dinosaurs first appeared on Earth.

Is that true? Or false?

It's TRUE.

There were huge trees. There were conifers (trees that bear pine cones) with trunks 10 feet in diameter. Some were 180 feet high. No grass, and no flowers yet.

But plenty of big trees.

When a dinosaur skull is found with the jaws wide open, we know that the dinosaur was eating at the time of death.

Is that right?

No. It's WRONG!

It doesn't show that at all.
In fact most skulls are found with jaws open.

Why is that?

After the dinosaur dies, the jaw muscles decay, and relax. This is what causes the mouth to flop open. It has nothing to do with whether or not the dinosaur was eating.

When the jaw is found closed, it could mean something else. Most likely a closed jaw means the skull was buried very soon after the dinosaur died. Covered up with earth, the jaw doesn't have space to flop open.

Is this true? Or false?

Scientists in several museums are now collecting dinosaur blood (which they obtained from fossilized mosquitos that had bitten dinosaurs).

As soon as they have enough dino-blood collected, they are going to start to try to create a living dinosaur by using the DNA in the blood.

Our government is firmly against this project because they say it is too dangerous.

FALSE!

How do we know?

First of all, no dinosaur blood has ever been found.

Second, you could have buckets of dinosaur blood, and, for many reasons, still not be able to create a dinosaur.

Finally, since there is no blood, and there is no such project, the government has no policy about it.

The biggest dinosaur skull ever found is:

(a) 3 feet wide and 4 feet high
(b) 5 feet wide and almost 6 feet high
(c) 10 feet wide and 8 feet high

The answer is: (c)!

Can you imagine a head that big?
But it's **TRUE!**

It was discovered in Montana. It is the skull of a ceratopsian — a horned dinosaur.

The discovery of two baby dinosaur skeletons inside two adult dinosaurs is proof that some dinosaurs gave birth to live babies, instead of laying eggs, as we once thought all dinosaurs did.

True? Or false?

FALSE!

Some time ago, in New Mexico, *Coelophysis* baby bones were found inside the body cavities of two adult *Coelophysis*. When the discovery was made, scientists wondered at first: Did this show that these dinosaurs were *viviparous* (animals that give birth to live young) instead of being *oviparous* (animals that lay eggs)?

If so, it would be a startling discovery.

But the answer was finally decided. It was NO.

How did they come to this decision?

First, by the size of the babies' bones. They were too big and too well-formed to be the bones of a baby developing inside the mother. Second, because the small pelvic opening — the birth canal — of *Coelophysis* was too small for babies of this size to fit through in birth. (Although it *was* big enough for an egg to pass through.)

How then did the babies get inside the adults?

You guessed it. They had been *eaten*. They were supper. They might have been eaten as carrion — that is, after they had already died.

Some dinosaurs protected their young by:

(a) carrying them piggyback

(b) spitting at their attackers

(c) having the young walk in the center of the herd, with the adults surrounding them

It's (c).

We have no way of knowing that dinosaurs carried their young piggyback — or "dinoback." Or that any dinosaurs spit at their enemies.

But we do know that adult sauropods surrounded the young ones when the herd was on the move.

How do we know this?

By footprints. We have found sets of prints with the larger ones at the outer edge of the group, and smaller prints of the young ones in the middle of the group.

The first dinosaurs ate lots of flowers.

True? Or false?

FALSE.

How do we know they didn't?

There *were* no flowers in the early days of dinosaurs. No grass, either. There were giant trees, and horsetails, and ferns, and bushes. But no flowers or grass. Flowering plants appeared only toward the end of the Age of Dinosaurs.

Dinosaur hunters are not too thrilled when they find dinosaur skulls because they find so many of them.

True? Or false?

FALSE!

They *are* thrilled to find a skull.

Why is that?

First of all, they do *not* find so many. Skulls are a rare find. Why is this?

The skull is often more fragile than most other bones. It breaks up easily. Possibly not many are found because predators crunched them to bits. In fact, the skull is probably the most valuable part of a dinosaur to find. Why?

Because it gives so much information about the dinosaur's way of life. It tells you the size of the brain, what the dinosaur ate (this from the teeth and jaws), and much more. This is what dinosaur expert John Horner says: "If I had only one part of an animal, I'd rather have a skull than anything else."

Which of these is true?

(a) Dinosaurs had a good sense of smell.

(b) Dinosaurs had keen hearing.

They're *both* TRUE.

How do we know?

The skulls tell us.

They had a large nasal opening, which is the sign of a keen sense of smell. And the way the ear bones are formed is a clue that dinosaurs' sense of hearing was good, too.

———————————

Many dinosaurs walked on tiptoe.

True? Or false?

It's TRUE.

How do we know?

We can tell this by the way the foot bones and ankle bones fitted together. *Iguanodon, Compsognathus, Tyrannosaurus,* ostrich dinosaurs, duckbill dinosaurs, and many others all walked on their toes.

It's not so unusual. Hippos and giraffes walk on their toes. Look at the dog's foot. Dogs are toe-walkers, too.

- Dog -

- Bear -

See how different a bear's foot is? It's flat on the ground. Not tippy-toe.

Lately we have been making so many dinosaur discoveries that dinosaur experts agree we have now discovered almost half of the different dinosaurs that ever existed. Maybe more.

Is this true? Or false?

It's FALSE.

Right now, we *are* finding "new" dinosaurs at a very fast rate. In fact, a "new" species is found about every seven weeks. Even so, we now know perhaps only two to five percent of dinosaurs that ever lived. That's what the experts tell us. Some say it's even less. Dinosaur expert John Horner says, "We probably don't know one percent of all species."

We will never know the complete dinosaur story. There are probably some types of dinosaurs that lived and died that we will never get to know about because there are no remains left of them. Or even if there *are* remains somewhere, we may never find them.

So there will always be blank spots in the dinosaur story that can never be filled in. But as time goes by, and more discoveries are made, we will certainly learn more about the dinosaur way of life. And bit by bit, as we fill in

some of the blanks, some things we now be-
lieve to be true may turn out to be false. And
some things we once never thought possible
could turn out to be true.

Index of Names